"*I Would Live For You* invites don't want to take - but do a Kate perfectly describe the collision of Glory and disaster exploding right before their very eyes - in the form of raw poetry, honest words, and thoughts inside of a brilliant mind, yet wounded body. Hanna's poetry will simultaneously wreck you and heal you - in ways that cannot be described in words - only feelings. Kate so carefully crafts her sister's thoughts into the most honest love letter to the reader leaving us with only one thought for certain; we are not alone in our suffering. *I Would Live For You* is as healing as it is beautiful. What do we do when God doesn't answer our prayers the way we think He should? Hanna will tell you that the answer is uncomfortable, yet satiated with Peace. Do you need peace in suffering today? Hanna and Kate show us the way."

Megan Faulkner, Author, Host of *Wife Me Up Podcast*, Youth Pastor

"You hold in your hands something sacred—groans that have arisen to the surface by one who had the courage to turn them into words. Honest words, tired words, frustrated words, hopeful words. May Hanna's laments, questions, and wrestling bring you the courage to be more honest about your suffering, but also about the God who is more kind and present than we often dare believe."

Kelly M. Kapic, author of *Embodied Hope: A Theological Meditation on Pain and Suffering*

"*I Would Live For You* captures the unbreakable bond of love in an exceptional family surrounding one of the bravest and most creative people I've ever met. This is a rare insight by her loving sister into her life and their loss."

Richard M. Gill, D.C.

"Hanna's words, wisdom, and ability to share her love, faith, and despair will fill your heart and give you courage. Hanna's deepest grief during her journey was her concern about the emptiness she knew we would feel. She hoped her poetry would bring us some comfort. It is a privilege to represent Hanna and her family in their fight for justice against Johnson & Johnson. Hanna's strength and fearless determination for justice will always inspire me."

Audrey Perlman Raphael, Partner at Levy Konigsberg LLP

"Every Memorial Day the CrossFit community (which is made up of less than 1% of the world's population) honors fallen Navy Lt. Murphy by completing one of the most intense workout circuits out there. Not only physically difficult but also mentally challenging— it's hard to find a friend who will do it with you. To my delight, I finally found the friend who said "Yes" to any challenge—Sweet Hanna.

We prayed and had a moment of silence before starting the workout; and Hanna reminded me that the weighted vest each participant wears during the workout is the exact amount of weight she lost after her first cancer surgery: 14lbs. With a smile, I threw on the vest. Throughout the intense journey of running miles, 100 push-ups, 200 pull-ups, and 300 squats, Hanna encouragingly whispered, "Keep going, Melis…"

Her grit was tenacious and her mental fortitude like no other! She was truly a warrior with a tender heart—pursuing life fearlessly. This book reveals how healing can be found in suffering. Through all of the intense physical pain, Hanna's heart reveals the hope for immortality and complete healing. She challenges us to hope for more than what we experience in the now. I am forever changed by her bravery, vulnerability, friendship, and faith in the Gospel."

Melissa Montalvo, CFP®, FAITH RX'D Chapter Leader CrossFit Guru, Lifelong Family Friend

"Strength, Honor, Dignity, Beauty, Responsibility, Talent, and Personality are just some of the words that describe the person of Hanna Wilt. It was my joy and privilege to have had a relationship with this incredible young woman for several years. A rare disease robbed her of long life, but the years she lived were full of happiness, laughter, accomplishment, and generosity. She loved her mother, her siblings, and her Lord and Savior with a rare sense of passion and commitment. She will always be remembered and loved by those of us who knew her and were honored to have been her friend. The pages that follow were written by her sister, Kate, and reflect all of the above."

Rev. Louis A. LaGatta, Executive Minister at Caleb International Ministries

"Hanna

My mind and body rest in the memories I carry with me.
My most treasured possessions.
Cherished, little, tiny moments.

Crop tops and high-waisted jeans that unabashedly revealed the fight fought
Short shorts and strong legs
Hair that changed color like a rainbow
Warm light and quiet calm
Japanese anime embodied as a Halloween ninja
A maker's heart
Infinite empathy and compassion
Nose rings and unbuttoned flannel shirts
Ineluctable beauty with the most exquisite smile
Life's barbarous habit of not knowing that the last time I saw you, would be the last time I saw you. Memories. The heart's sublime embodiment of cherished moments we shared together.
With strength.
With love.
Hanna."

Hope Bailey, Maker at Hope + Mary

I Would Live For You

A Young Poet's Walk through Grief and Acceptance
of Her Terminal Cancer Diagnosis

Hanna Wilt

Edited and Woven Together by Her Sister, Kate Kiesel

Copyright © 2023 Hanna Wilt

All writing is permissible to share by readers across all social platforms only if the writer is credited:
@hannawilt / Hanna Wilt
@iwouldliveforyoubook

All rights reserved. No part of this book may be used or reproduced in any manner whatsoever without written permission from the editor, except in the case of brief quotations embodied in articles and reviews. This book is not permitted for resale/wholesale unless a direct agreement has been made with the editor. For wholesale inquiries please contact the editor via hannawilt.com

ISBN (print): 978-1-955051-13-2
ISBN (eBook): 978-1-955051-14-9

Published in association with Punchline Agency LLC.

Editor:
Kate Kiesel
katekiesel.com

Designer:
Kristin McNess Moran
kristinmcnessmoran.com

Cover Painting:
Michael J. Johnson, *Noli Timere - Be Not Afraid*, 2022
Michaeljohnson.studio

Scripture quotations marked TPT are from The Passion Translation*. Copyright 2017, 2018, 2020 by Passion & Fire Ministries, Inc. Used by permission. All rights reserved. ThePassionTranslation.com.

For my Mom

Thank you for walking me home.

FOREWORD

By Kate

My sister Hanna, the author of this book, went home to Heaven at the age of 27 on Valentine's Day, February 14, 2022. She went home after years of being at war—body, mind, and spirit—with one of the most wicked cancers no one has ever heard of: abdominal mesothelioma. This type of cancer develops in the thin layers of tissue lining the abdomen. The disease took root in her body after years of using Johnson & Johnson Baby Powder, poisoning her with asbestos found in the talc powder. This is another level of evil, one I strongly suggest you research on your own time.

My family and I walked alongside and witnessed our Hanna as she went through loss after loss after loss of her life here on Earth. You see, what we learned is that dying is not the only heartache that comes with a terminal diagnosis. What's almost more earth-shattering is the multitude of deaths that happen along the way home. And for anyone reading this that is walking through a terminal illness diagnosis or walking alongside that of a loved one, my family grieves with you.

—

In the past five years our family has gone through an intense season of loss. My younger brother, Sam, and his wife, Melissa, lost their first child, Emilia, during birth. Our parents separated. Our father, Bruce, was diagnosed with Non-Hodgkin's Lymphoma. After being told it was highly curable, he collapsed one day and was in intensive care unable to communicate until passing three weeks later. And most recently, we lost our sweet Hanna, the youngest girl in our family of six kids.

To say our perception of life has been rocked is an understatement. Blown to pieces is more like it.

We believe that Emilia, Bruce, and Hanna are all home with Jesus; that they are now and forever healthy and strong, full of life in their glorified bodies. We don't believe in Heaven as a form of escapism from the sorrow of this world, rather we believe it informs how we view life and live here on earth, because God promises we will be with Him when our earthly bodies pass away. We believe because all things beautiful and good on earth point us to the place He prepares for us. Author Peter Kreeft puts it so perfectly when he writes, "Earth was Heaven's womb, Heaven's nursery, Heaven's dress rehearsal. Heaven was the meaning of the earth."[1] May we live like we believe that.

—

Hanna and I regularly shared our artwork with each other, using our respective crafts as means to seek the Lord while encouraging each other along the way. She, the poet, I, the weaver. I watched her journey from writing and keeping her poems secret to agreeing to display them in a community art show at my old studio, to sitting around my mom's living room reading her most intimate writing out loud to her family and best friend. I think that's how art-making starts for all of us, in the secret place. And how perfectly that mirrors the secret place in which we seek the Lord when no one is there to see. The secret place cannot be forgone, it is the birthing place.

And like our relationship with the Lord, it's vital we share the light of our art with the world. I do believe there are times to make art as a form of private worship and not share it publicly, but for the most part, we need to share with others what we make. A friend of mine and wildly talented painter, Michael Johnson (he painted the cherry blossoms on the cover of this book!), once told me he believes that a work of art is not complete until it is shared with someone, inviting the viewer to connect with and have a response to the piece. So good and true and often hard to do.

---

[1] Kreeft, *Everything You Have Ever Wanted to Know about Heaven— But Never Dreamed of Asking*, 17.

It's intimidating to be vulnerable and share our art with people. I still struggle with it sometimes— usually with the pieces I'm most called to share publicly. But I've learned that you soon realize that our stories, our intentions, our gifts are all so incredibly different and each piece has its own purpose in the world— and that's to be respected. We can't keep the gifts and messages God's given us all to ourselves, there are people waiting to receive the blessing and healing we carry.

Months before Hanna passed, we started working on this book together. I believe it carries a special and timely anointing, not only because of my intimate connection to its author, but because I am so passionate about the way God speaks to us and brings healing through art making and viewing. It was a dream of hers to publish her poetry, one she felt was too late to carry out, leaving her heartbroken that she "never got the chance to leave a legacy behind" (her words). Little did she know, do we all know really, that it's our lives that are the legacy we leave behind. And she left behind a more beautiful and powerful legacy than extra years on earth could ever promise a person. Even still, I felt the call to weave what was on her heart and in her notebooks together and help her create what she so desperately sought during her journey—a way to let people know they are not alone in their suffering.

I learned from Hanna that being diagnosed with a terminal illness is incredibly lonely. I believe it was especially lonely for her because she was so young, leaving this world at the age of 27. While her peers were pregnant with dreams and possibilities for their futures, she was undergoing massively traumatic surgeries that left her unable to conceive or dream—struggling just to breathe, eat and go to the bathroom normally. But regardless of age, suffering is so often a very lonely wilderness. Most people simply avoid another's suffering. They stop calling. They don't stop by. They wince and turn and walk away. To walk beside someone in their suffering is a costly but precious gift.

I don't know the depths and despair of what she went through, of what you may be going through right now. I am so grateful for how willing she was to let us get close to her in her suffering, because in her vulnerability and absolute honesty she showed us a grace and a love and a purity that points only to Jesus being with her in the fire. It was messy and horrific and traumatizing, and it was so beautiful. Until the end, I prayed for and truly believed that Hanna could be healed of her disease. And though her physical body was not healed this side of Heaven, I know that I witnessed the healing of her heart and soul because of her honesty and openness to the Lord through it all. In the fire, Hanna became who she was created to be all along, before the trauma and pain and death entered into her life. She was free from all of the lies that get put on us or that we pick up along the way. It was the most intense tension between joy and sorrow I've ever witnessed as we sat in our mom's living room joking that she was "finally in her prime" (her words) and then weeping with disappointment that she'd be leaving us so soon.

I believe that what you hold in your hands is something sacred, written on holy ground (yes, a cozy bed can be holy), breathed on by the Spirit of God, spoken to my sister in whispers and shouts along her pilgrimage. As Hanna got closer to leaving this world; when she could no longer eat or drink anything without immediately and violently vomiting it up, when she would wake up in the middle of the night in excruciating pain, unable to sleep because the tumors were taking over her insides and leaving no room for her few remaining organs, she would write. I would go to sleep with my 4-month-old baby in a room down the hall and wake up in the morning to text messages from Hanna with some of the most beautiful writing she ever did. The veil was thin and she carried love letters straight from Heaven.

In these pages you will find a friend in Hanna. A friend who's gone before you and now sits down beside you to say, "I know. You don't have to be brave anymore." A friend whose testimony will share with you a Grace and a Hope and a Peace that surpasses all understanding, which makes no sense to the natural world because none of those things are of this world. They won't be shared with you in some sort of "suffering to success" story— Hanna would say that is the absolute worst, only she'd say it more explicitly to express just how much she hated it. She will make you laugh.

Instead, you will find a friend that is beautifully and brutally honest, open and willing to go to the places so many of us avoid. One who sits in truth and holds space for the uncomfortable. One who writes openly about suffering, despair, loss and grief; and of hope, reconciliation, love and life. One who loved the ocean and poetry and flowers and food and people and knew that to create beauty in collaboration with our Creator is often the most defiant act of rebellion against the evil of death. This friend you'll find in Hanna, she kept company with Christ through the art of poetry, and this collection of poems was written for you.

Kate Kiesel
Darmstadt, Germany
October, 2022

CONTENTS

Introduction by Hanna ... ix

Part One: *You Seem like Someone Who Cries in Secret a Lot* ... 1

Part Two: *Have You Ever Praised God from a Hospital Bed?* ... 31

Part Three: *Efflorescence: A State of Blooming, Flowering, and Development* ... 51

Part Four: *What's inside Me Never Dies* ... 81

Therapeutic Writing Exercise: *An Encouragement to Create from Kate* ... 107

About the Authors ... 127

We Would Love to Connect with You ... 128

Kate's Gratitudes ... 131

A Note from the Cover Artist ... 133

About the Women Who Helped Bring This Book to Life ... 135

Bibliography ... 137

INTRODUCTION

By Hanna

I HAVE ALWAYS BELIEVED THAT THE PURPOSE OF US creating is to externalize what we are experiencing internally in order to make sense of it. Art allows us to interpret life in a way that makes it both accessible and tangible to those around us. We create because of the innate need to connect and feel less alone, if only we can be brave enough to allow ourselves to both wither and bloom within that process. Sometimes what we make is a mess (as are we), while every now and then, something magical emerges that allows us that moment of satisfaction to say "this is what I meant all along." I believe art is a selfless act—one that takes what's on the inside and puts it out in the world for others to connect to and feel seen. Only when we are brave enough to fail are we then able to, hopefully, create something reflective of ourselves and gift that unwinding of our hearts to the world.

Even in these last few months of my life, I can feel myself being cracked open and unwound to a degree I'm not sure I can ever fully describe. What I'm learning is that to truly share our stories, we need a lot of help. It's in receiving that help that this dream of mine may finally come to fruition and bloom at last. I'm learning the importance of connection and vulnerability not just in the final product, but actually how vital it is for the parts of the product to come together in the first place. We serve a God whose biggest promise to us is that He will never forsake us and is with us every step of the way. Why wouldn't this be reflective in the creation that we make to imitate the ultimate Creator that knitted us within our mother's womb? That may be one of the most important lessons that I have learned in these past few years—that I cannot do any of this on my own, and that true love and connection are found in accepting the reality of my limitations.

Just like the cherry blossom tree, I only need to bloom at just the right time; and though winter may come again and again, those that love me will be there to show me the direction back to my spring once again. It is my wish that those that read this work too may find their own beauty in their limitations, and see how we serve a Father that welcomes that neediness and brokenness with open arms every step of the way, if only we allow ourselves the grace and honesty to be the messy beings we so often are ashamed of. May these words help you find your way back to your spring despite the harshness of life's winters.

Hanna Wilt

January 29, 1995 - February 14, 2022

Part One

You Seem like Someone Who Cries in Secret a Lot

The way I would describe my relationship with God is as a series of immense softenings within myself, ones that entailed a giving up of my control and an acknowledgment that I don't always have to be strong and put together. These time periods in my life have been extremely painful, disarming, and destabilizing—but in the process, they have revealed to me a sense of peace in the midst of a storm, and have taught me to be able to let go of the delusional concept of complete control and the belief that we are the masters of our own fate. I will not say that this has been easy, that I have not at times clawed at what I want to keep within my grasp as it has been ripped from me. But what I will say is that despite how heartbreaking much of this experience has been, it has allowed me to come to one of the most important understandings I could ever ask for: that no matter what I do, God will not abandon me, and that I am not alone because He is walking right beside me through it all.

I was diagnosed with Abdominal Peritoneal Mesothelioma a few months after waking up one morning with such bad pain in my lower right abdomen that I couldn't even walk normally. This morning began about a two-month process of hospital visits, to an eventual surgery to remove ovarian cysts. To me, everything had gone smoothly, and I was going to return back to school shortly to finish my senior year of college—never could I have anticipated the conversation I was going to have only five days later.

I was walking downstairs when I saw everyone in my family sitting in the living room, and my mom said to me: "I need to talk to you, they found something during surgery." I felt my heart drop through the floor, and I immediately knew what that meant: I had cancer. I began sobbing, as did the rest of my family, which only led to my sister nervously blurting out "Mom said you can get a dog!" which helped me to stop crying for a few seconds, but the tears quickly resumed. I can remember thinking, "Lord I can't do this, please don't make me do this," and how scared I was of what lay ahead of me. For the next two weeks, my stomach would drop constantly throughout the day as the reality of my situation would hit me again and again and again; the sadness I felt was all-consuming.

The initial stages of something like cancer are really confusing. There's the process of letting people know and dealing with their weird responses, which often can be pretty insensitive and confusing. Then there are the doctor appointments across the country, where you each time get to re-experience what it feels like to be diagnosed with cancer. The doctors will confirm the diagnosis, you'll sit there as they tell you your statistics, then they'll go through their prognosis, which consists of a terrifying explanation of the chemo and surgery they have planned and the different possibilities of what organs will have to be removed as well as what life could potentially look like after cancer treatment. In my case, the doctors wanted to hit me quickly, and they wanted to hit me hard. That meant they wanted to do extensive chemo before and after surgery, with a surgery that would consist of the most invasive cut I could get, removal of multiple organs, including my female organs, and the potential to never fully recover back to my previous potential. Oh, and there's still the possibility that my cancer will come back. The decisions that I was forced to make during that time are ones that I hope none of you ever have to experience, and it truthfully was a long process for me to be able to go through what needed to be done. In five months time, my condition severely declined. I was sleeping constantly, had fevers almost every night, and my stomach was becoming more and more distended. What we had been doing was not working, so it was time to re-evaluate and come up with a new plan. We had tried multiple different routes and everything we could to not have to go through with the worst possibility– the 9-hour surgery I just described , but in the end, it was unavoidable.

To have struggled with my faith the way I did during this time I believe is only natural, though uncomfortable and something we don't always like to talk about or acknowledge. Initially, there was fear, which then turned into anger. I was so angry with God—that He would let something like this happen to me. I had upended everything in my life, started completely from scratch in obedience to Him, moved across the country away from everything that was comfortable to start my life over here at Covenant, and worked so hard to become a better, healthier version of myself. And, honestly, I was doing a pretty good job. I understood that to follow Christ requires giving up what you think your life should look like and allowing God to shape it to what He knows is best for you, and that this process is an extremely uncomfortable thing. To follow Christ is a giving up of our own control, and I had been working hard to do that—to say "not my will, but yours Lord." So why, then, had He allowed me to have cancer?

Untitled

You cracked open my chest
and rib by rib
I was drained

I begged you to stop
crying out
"Lord, why must it hurt so bad?"

My child

a surgeon must first cut open its patient to reach the dying organ if there is to be healing

At first you must suffer a while

I am making you new

Spring

If I have ever seen enough,
If I have ever felt enough,
If I have ever cried enough,
Then I, in this moment surrounding us, have lived.
I, at this time, am enough.

* * *

God bless the way the world takes,
so that I may give.

God bless the pits I have been thrown into—
that, at times, have thrown myself into;
For surely, a garden grew thereafter.

God bless the things that have wrecked me—
for the ways my ribcage has been stretched out wide
to expose beating, bleeding flesh—
For only then,
at that time,
have those ribbed-wings taken flight.

The same suffering that suffocates
gives breath to a new life.
Birthing pains not meant to bear alone;
though, when shared,
become more like growing pains than
an unburdened body;
more like being pulled under than
a lightened load.

Either way, my legs won't stop aching.
But isn't that the point?

Tell me,
is sorrow sweeter when shared?
What is that twisting in your heart
that feels like a key turning in a lock?
It tears soft tissue either way it goes.

Tell me,
What is it that makes you want to whisper your words to them
— no, makes you want to scream them
so that everyone I have ever loved
may take ribcage-flight too;
which, at most times, is everyone.
Either way, my legs still ache.

* * *

I saw when the flowers bloomed.
When you saw me as I was,
I looked away.
When you saw me as I could be,
I ran the other way.
I cried when the flowers bloomed,
and you taught me what it meant to be loved.

I cry when the flowers bloom.
I am learning that that is enough.

21

It's been 21 years that my bones have been aching,
scratching from inside my chest to be released.
Marrow screaming for sweet relief,
you quieted my wallowing blood.

Being hurt is not beautiful,
but there is something beautiful in the rawness that comes with the experience of the pain.
An uprooting of an oak tree planted 21 years ago,
I've been using a blunt shovel for far too long.

I'm still trying to figure out if it's strong to want to love,
or if it's weak to shut it out—
because I have spent 21 years loathing that desire in me,
and I'm exhausted.
And I am calm;
and I am at peace.

Untitled

A predetermined destiny of purposelessness,
a wandering
wondering what's next.

Melancholy at its most high;
Tell me, how many times have you felt that itch in the back of your throat?
A fire aching from your knees to the back of your skull—
a dull pain, as they tap, tap, tap on your temple.

How do you learn to clear your lungs when you've been suffocating yourself for 21 years?
'Cause I wanna breathe in deeply,
but not really,
because oxygen only fuels that fire that's been itching
since they first started tapping.

So instead,
I will clear my throat
and keep on wandering.

Wisteria

I wish to hang amongst the vines of the wisteria.
Hidden from your harsh words
and gritted teeth;
to lay softly within the sweet smells
of a type of comfort I have denied I needed.
I want the vines to tangle around my limbs,
as petals caress open my ribs.
Alas, exposing what you have taught me to hide.

Untitled

I'm still trying to figure out which hurt more
You sat there
as I regurgitated
the parts of my youth so deep;

my intestines splayed out in front of us—
I cried to you
as you loved me.

Emilia

We all have a tail.
So does he,
as does she.
Though this one in particular,
follows a group of three.

I want to hug my brother.
I want to hold my sister.
I want to cut off their tail that seems to drag a bit longer than others
I have seen.
I want to kiss my niece.
I want to right what seems wrong.

But I forget:
That I am not the maker of their story.
That I had not woven that little *esperanza* in my sister's belly.
That, sometimes, our tale is one of pain and suffering.

And still, I forget:
That in these days of trouble,
there is shelter.
That in this beating, aching chest,
there is love.
That in a woman's womb,
there is grace.

And so, I honor you both, dear brother and sister—
As you have worn your tale with dignity and grace,
while I have tried to shed mine.

For you have kept soft that beating thing that aches so deep,
while I have hardened mine.
For you have continued to speak love,
while I have remained silent.
May these words be my apology and my thank you.

I am sorry,
for my silence and fear.
And I thank you,
for inviting me into this beautifully painful, perfect, and raw gift that is,
Emilia.

Untitled

Mother, tell what you see
when you take a look at me.
All along, all along—
these have been cooking in me
for far too long.

Untitled

Lately I've been playing my music really loud
We are so defined by our pain and we don't even know it
We are begging
Literally begging
To be loved
to be seen
And we don't even know it
Let me tell you my story
Rip open this cage in my chest
And let this bird stretch its wings
Can you see me?
We ache for something so deep
And we can't even comprehend what
Do you see me now?
We try to turn it down
No turn it off
By turning up the volume
Turning on the things that will turn it all off
Cause maybe if I can't hear it then I'll stop feeling it
Cause if you can't see me
I don't wanna hear myself
And we don't even know it
Share with me your story

Untitled

I see you struggle
and I want you to know that
I love you for it.

Untitled

What would you do if I told you how I felt?
Would you implode into yourself,
fearing the damage that can be done when the truth is set free—
you would shut me out.

Or would you blossom into the person you've always had within you?
The most beautiful flower I ever laid eyes on;
the love you set up on a shelf so long ago finally taken down—
welcomed like a long awaited birth,
like the warmth of an embrace you've been craving even before that realization.

But the thought of asking for it only turns you inside out;
puts on display all that's hidden in that cavity within your ribs—
invites in the purest form of pain.

Let me ask to give you that warmth instead.

Untitled

Is it fair for me to want more from myself?
Is it fair for me to want to win every battle I'm thrown into?
I like to think it is

Sometimes all I want
is to give all that I am
to everyone I love
but, I swear to God
I'm so selfish,
and
I swear to God,
I'm so tired,
that I just end up being angry
or disappointed
or maybe, a bit of both
or maybe, I was just angry to begin with

cause I hate that my dad never called me—
that I had to call him
But I hate more
that I wasn't even surprised,
that I couldn't even let myself
be disappointed.

And I hate the way my sister
said she was sick of it being about me
even though
I was the one who was sick
that she hated me when we were little

but somehow
she was the one hurt by her hatred
and did you know how painful it was when
I was told to shut up
when I didn't want to stand in front of the church
on mother's day
soon your womb would be warm
yet mine will forever remain bare

I hate that I'm not allowed to feel
how fucking bad it hurt
how that agony
still lingers
just like this scar
down my middle
the top is where my anger is born
the bottom, my sorrow
follow the curvature with me
to help me understand
why it is
I can't escape whatever it is
I'm trying to give birth to
'Cause I can't seem to unravel
all the ways they stitched me up

I hate the ways my youth
has been slowly stripped from me;
how, at times, felt more like,
a limb ripped from its socket

And I hate how much
I fucking hate these things in me

I just want to get back to the part
where we talk about how much
I want to love, love, love
to kiss the eyelids
of that child
whose father didn't call
all the while i'll sing to them:
"sweet child, stay a child,
you don't have to grow up so fast
dear baby, lovely fawn
keep your limbs attached"

Untitled

How am I supposed to give a shit
when the void my body was created around
no longer will bring forth the void of another
What am I to fill it with now?

I swear
if one more woman offers me her womb
as if she is my Savior
I will revoke the faith she expects of me
I will deny her as Peter did
but will not ask for such forgiveness
Do not think your gifts are ones that I want
when you cannot begin to breathe in the reality
that strangles me
— my pain did not ask for your charity
do not force your way into a door
of which you have no access to

Untitled

I am telling you
You do not know sorrow
Until you have mourned the loss of the creation that resides within you
Till you have cried over what could have been
But is now snatched inside out from you

Untitled

Some days
it feels like this grief will swallow me whole
Some days
I want it to

Untitled

I want to know what it means to live
To not scratch, rather, claw at this suit of flesh constantly
I want to end this war with my body
I want to breathe
This is me raising my white flag
in hopes my insides will return the gesture
That my organs and I will embrace lovingly
may we reach that peace of our youth
once again
Let us eat watermelon on a summer day
without fear of the hellfire it could be feeding
Let us run to feel the capacity of our lungs
without the aching of numb toes and a faint head
Let us talk with the world once again
not about this struggle
but of books, flowers, the weather, I don't know
anything
anything but this
No more "how are you feeling"'s
No more "you don't even look sick"'s
No more "yeah but it's only for a time"'s
Cause I'm exhausted
I'm aching
And I'm mourning a loss
This is not the body of a 22 year old
This is the body of someone fighting a war

Untitled

Even if you don't come to a resolution, just the very act of entering into honest conversation about God and who He is, and to wrestle with honesty those deepest struggles allows for God to enter into the hurts and begin to bring peace in them in ways you can't experience when you keep them constantly hidden or denied.

A Love Song to Who I Once Was (And Still Am)

This is the fight where you're fighting for yourself—
fighting to not lose yourself—
a reclamation of sorts,
or maybe just part of the ontogenesis.
Cause while the world will be gnashing at you,
trying to reduce you to nothing,
You are going to have to find it within your being
to bear your teeth back.
An unapologetic presence,
a confidence in the existence of those things that once were,
still are.

My love, my heart.
From within you has come great, beautiful things—
and even greater things to come—
Because you've had your veins ripped from you,
and you kept breathing regardless.
Fight on, my breath.

I'll Read This to You When You're Ready

There are about
216 words that I want to tell you
by the end of this day.

Words like: the way you laugh makes my chest feel full,
makes my feet feel grounded, makes my voice feel shaky—
makes me scared to breathe out of fear of what will be born of such breath.

His laugh rips poetry from my lungs.

I want to write you poem after poem
I want to call you babe

I want to go back in time and let that little boy know
that one day a little girl will see the way you fight,
and know it's because you're scared.
She'll be scared too.

When's the last time someone told you
that you were meant for sweet and tender things?

I hope one day you let me share this with you.

One day I hope to no longer rip forth these words,
sticky on my ribs—
but instead,
for you to wipe them cleanly off,
so that I may pour them into you.

I hope one day you are ready to hear all 216 words.
But if loving you means waiting,
then I will swallow the words that fill my chest,
'till you are ready to hear
what your laugh has inspired.

Untitled

I'm still waiting for this pain to come to fruition
For this suffering to have meaning
Even if it's for someone else
Because, my God
Some days
My ribs feel so heavy
Like the time they burned the inside of my diaphragm
so I could keep on eating and breathing
Even though
Sometimes
I don't want to

Untitled

I don't want to talk
I'm not ready yet to tell people about what just happened
How could I, when I don't even understand it myself

Part Two

Have You Ever Praised God from a Hospital Bed?

At first, I believed that I was holding on to my youth and health too tightly, and that God was trying to teach me to let go of something that I cared about too much. I have heard this kind of thing from a lot of people before—where they think God is punishing them for loving something too much, so He takes it away, whether it be a job, a friendship, a significant other, and so on. To any of you that have felt this way before, I want you to hear me when I say this: God is not that insecure. Yes, God is a jealous God, and He is jealous for your love, but that doesn't mean He destroys anything that gets in the way of you and Him. He wants you to choose to love Him more than other things in life, otherwise He wouldn't have given us free will, because what is love if it's not a decision that you made? What I think is actually happening in these situations—where we think God is punishing us—is that suffering and pain exposes our weaknesses, and our weaknesses expose the things we care about the most. So, in a case of losing a friend, maybe it's just that you rely too much on the affirmation of your relationships to believe you are worthy of love, rather than knowing that God loves you no matter what you do. In my case, I was scared to let go of the control of my own body and my life, because I have felt like all my life nothing has ever been stable or safe. I was afraid to put everything on the line and trust God, because I wasn't so sure if this God could be trusted.

In that fear of giving up myself, I struggled to find purpose in it all. Such a battle for my life felt meaningless, like there was nothing to be fighting for. I felt like a part of me had already died, and I was terrified that God was asking too much of me. I looked at myself and thought, "what could possibly be worth so much loss and suffering?" I did not feel like I had the strength or faith to trust God with my life, to believe that He would take care of me and that He had good things for my life. Therefore, there was no purpose for me to keep struggling through it all. I had gone from a strong, healthy 22-year-old, about to be a senior in college, a captain on the Track team, graduate with my friends, and so on, to now living back at home and isolated from my community, being exhausted just by walking up the steps, and afraid that any mistake I made would only make my cancer worse. I felt like everything had gone backwards, that none of my hard work had been worth it, and I was so mad that God had let this happen. But it was also during this time that I learned the importance of the church and the community around you. I learned how it's okay to not see the purpose in your suffering and to be mad at God, because God can handle your anger. It's okay to not believe or pray sometimes, because that's where the church steps in to pray and believe for you. And my church at home did just that. I was blessed enough to have an entire body of believers love me and believe enough for me that God would take care of me, that slowly but surely, I was eventually able to see that for myself, though this process was slow. I am so thankful too for the people I know I had praying for me at Covenant College, and especially Dr. Kapic, who consistently emailed me to tell me he was praying for me, who didn't try to make sense of my suffering, but instead helped me to not feel alone, and always answered my long (and often very emotional) emails. And I am thankful to all the staff and teachers were willing to walk through this process with me, as anyone who has dealt with cancer before knows, it's something that is a part of your life forever.

It was also during this time that I learned what it meant to be thankful and present in the day you are in. If I was able to work out a little one day, then I did so. If I sat on the couch all day playing Zelda on my Nintendo Switch, then I was content with the option to be able to be distracted from my situation that day. I learned to let myself be angry, to be sad, to be joyful— to let everyday just be whatever it needed to look like. I learned to be thankful that I had a home to live in, that I had a mother and family to come home to, a mother that walked through it with me every single step of the way. I gave my mom a mother's day card last year that said "without you, I'd literally be dead." It's obviously a joke on how your mother gave birth to you, but for me, it was in the literal sense of how my mother took care of me while I was sick. Having cancer and being so sick, you need someone in your corner to fight for you, because honestly, sometimes you can't fully acknowledge the reality of the situation and that you could potentially die. I am blessed enough that I had a mother that fought tooth and nail for me. Thank you, Mom.

God's presence in the last month or so before my surgery was undeniable, and at last, I began to be able to stop fighting Him. One night while driving by the beach back home after the gym, in the stillness of the night and being alone, I became so overwhelmingly aware of God's closeness to me, like a wave that rushed over me, and I felt Him say "we go until we can go no more." I pulled over in front of the ocean, and I wept for what I was going to have to do, and I wept in the understanding that God was going to be there with me every step of the way. At last, I gave it all up, and I said, "Okay, I can do this." I wept because I finally understood what it meant to not be alone.

My surgery in total took nine hours, in which my spleen, uterus, an ovary, my appendix, part of large intestines, and my greater omentum were removed, which was then followed by HIPEC treatment in which they completely saturate your abdominal cavity for 90 minutes with heated chemotherapy. I remember waking up finally and there were wires and tubes coming out from everywhere. A few days in, I got into an argument with a nurse when I threatened to pull out my NG tube cause it kept making me cough, which is super fun when your stomach muscles have just been cut in half.

That time in the hospital, and even following when I got home, I didn't know it was possible to experience such pain. I couldn't do anything myself as the simplest tasks exhausted me, and my body had just been completely traumatized. I slept in my mom's room for two months, and it was three months before I could sleep on my side again without it feeling like my rib cage was getting crushed. I was constantly exhausted, had to relearn how to eat and digest my food, and was a whopping 118 pounds. I can remember looking in the mirror and crying because I didn't recognize the girl looking back at me. The now 23-year-old girl who had worked so hard was no longer there in my eyes, and I felt as though I had completely lost myself. Literally everything had been stripped away, and all that I was left with was my existence. This, for me, was a revelatory thing. How do I still find myself worthy of love and necessary enough to exist if I can no longer be the Hanna I have always been? Where do I find my sense of self when it feels like all that I am has been ripped away, leaving just a shell of a girl that barely exists in the space that she occupies, especially when that existence itself is so painful?

This process of re-finding myself has taken an extremely long time, but I think I was able to do it in a way that began first with the understanding that I am worthy because I am God's, and not because of any sort of expectations that some one or myself put on me. My time having to not only look death in the eyes, but also embrace that possibility gave me a profound understanding of the lack of control of something that is taken for granted by all of us on a daily basis—

that at any point in time, this could be our last breath. I am able to go forward because I can take it a day at a time, and because I know that ultimately, I am not the one in control. To have your very life be put into the hands of God in such an in-your-face way, you can't help but be changed by it. When I had my first scan to see if they had gotten all the disease, there was a moment a few days before where I thought to myself "Even if I'm just buying more time, it all has been worth it." That is the peace that I can experience when I am able to give up my life to God and know that He is taking care of me.

In the beginning of the book of Job, we see Job lamenting his birth and questioning the point of his existence. He states in Chapter 6: "What is my strength, that I should wait?/ And what is my end, that I should be patient?" Then later in 7 he says "I loathe my life; I would not live forever./ Leave me alone, for my days are a breath." I was reading through it the other day and honestly, I started laughing, not because it was funny, but because I have felt this exact way. This feeling of questioning and existential crisis is so rampant and important enough to address that it's right here in scripture. I am comforted by the honesty in which Job struggles, and as we know, Job is no stranger to suffering. In Kurt Vonnegut's book *Slaughterhouse Five*, the main character, Billy Pilgrim, is in the veteran's hospital to heal from war injuries after being a prisoner. Every time his mother comes to visit Billy, Billy hides beneath his bed sheets and won't talk or look at her. His mother keeps on trying to get him to respond, but to no avail, and so she leaves. The story goes on to tell us that it wasn't because Billy resented his mother that he ignored her, but it was because she was the one who gave him life, and he was ashamed because, often, he didn't feel grateful to be alive. This shame I think is something we often don't talk about in the Christian community, and it is one that I really struggled with, and still do. I'll feel like I'm ungrateful or like I'm selfish because of how hard life can feel at times—that I'm not sure how much more grief I can carry around with me. But then you read through scripture, and all of a sudden you're confronted with all this pain and suffering and questioning—and the answer we're met with is a God that saves us by dying for us.

I don't think we can begin to comprehend God's love and grace until we allow ourselves to confront the difficult questions like pain and suffering. If we constantly pull our bed sheets over our head, we cut ourselves off from the opportunity to experience God showing up in the ways He promises to. Rather than just vapidly stating scripture, because that's what Sunday school taught us, we are able to step into the truth of it and say, "That is true and my life is a reflection of that." We are able to see that thankfulness and joy doesn't look like always being happy and saying thank you all the time, but rather, it looks like reverence for a God that calls us child, sacrifices His son so we can be with Him, and give us His Spirit so that He may dwell in us. We can't heal until we are first honest with ourselves and with God, because I hate to break it to you, but He already knows what you're thinking. It's just when you're honest with Him that He says finally "I can work with this."

This past February, my father died from Non-Hodgkin's Lymphoma. Over the span of three weeks, he was admitted to ICU and then passed away. Going home and spending a week and a half in the hospital, literally watching my father die in front of me, I couldn't help but be brought back to my own experience and struggle with cancer—the beeping IV monitors, the sterile smell of the hospital, the way the hospital gowns snap by the shoulders—it was all so familiar because less than a year ago, that was me. Life has continuously broken my heart, and at times, it has felt agonizing to look at the reality of it all that is splayed out in front of me. This time around though with my dad, there wasn't even an attempt to not try to feel the pain and grief of it all. I allowed myself to melt into what was aching, to cry as I saw I needed, and in the process, love my family around me as they grieved too. What I saw happen during these weeks and the following ones was something I think I can honestly say I've never seen in my family before. My family that had once been so divided, with parents in the process of getting a divorce, was now altogether holding one another, as we each took our turn to mourn. What I saw in all of us was grace, in such a beautiful way that I don't even know how to put it into words. And this, I believe, is one of the paradoxical things about God—that in the most painful times of mourning, there can be this wild exchange of love and joy that simultaneously exists when we decide to love despite how bad we are hurting. Suffering and joy are not opposites, but can both exist in the same moment in a way that I think only grace allows, and I think part of that comes when we stop trying to make sense of it all and just let the situation be what it is. When we let go of the delusion that we have it all together and we have ultimate control, we allow space for God to step in and give us the gift of peace that comes with the understanding that He is right there in the pits with us.

Untitled

I want someone to ask me about it
Before I forget how it felt

Do we ever actually recover?

I want to communicate
what it all felt like
I want to scream out everything
the way it felt
when my insides wanted out
more times than I can count
So much so
that I hated the lady puking
in the room next to mine
I hated her drama
and retching
But, mostly,
I hated the way
she projectile vomited
the truth
all over my hospital gown
I hated how I was her,
and she was me.
I hated how openly she shared
our embodied misery
I hated how I recognized myself
in the way
she projectile vomited
our truth,
all over my hospital gown
the way she said,
"I know you see me"
as I turned up Lauryn Hill
in my headphones
and sang softly to myself

Untitled

I have felt consumed for my entire life
Overwhelmed with the awareness of it all
I do not wish to taste
The enormity of my existence
Any longer
For it aches too deep
And it thrills too euphorically
I forgot what it means to be alive
Until I get to love again
But I also am reminded
Of what it means to feel like you're dying
So, rather, I wish to choose to not be consumed

Untitled

I have felt what it is to have your body suffocate itself
Yet here I am, still breathing

Untitled

I've realized that
all anyone really wants
is for someone to acknowledge their pain
To come up beside me while I lay in bed
curl up and hold me,
maybe kiss my head,
and say
"None of this is fair,
you don't have to pretend like it's okay anymore"

Untitled

If all else,
I wanna remain soft
despite the way
it makes me bleed more easily
See, my parents are getting divorced
But watching my mom
hold that cup of water
for my dad in his hospital bed
felt like grace

Untitled

I am
50 percent of the ashes that lay before me

Untitled

Because there's a little boy in the father
And there's a little girl in the mother
And there's a child that's within their daughter
That's been hiding away for too long

Untitled

And I felt guilt for the absence of my appreciation for the things that kept me whole for half of my life

Untitled

I feel like my life has been one huge competency trip in which I've been proving I don't need anyone, and now that I'm acknowledging I do, it's pretty dismantling

Untitled

I find myself wanting to connect
with parts of you
now that you're gone

Untitled

So much crying, but still so much laughter.
So much grief, but still so much joy and gratitude.
My family has been (and is still going) through a lot this year. Even so, in the moments of the deepest heartache, we continue to hold one another in our weaknesses as we each take our turn grieving and confronting what hurts.
In my times of greatest desperation, God keeps showing me how not alone I really am. I just have to let myself be broken.
Lord, give me the grace to remain soft no matter where my steps lead to.

Part Three

Efflorescence: A State of Blooming, Flowering, and Development

As painful as this has all been, I have found that these moments of suffering allow us to see more clearly the profound and simple beauty that exists around us. In fact, it has allowed me to live more simply in general, because it has shown me what is actually important and what matters in this life. People matter. Honesty matters. Loving one another matters. Every single one of you matters, and there is meaning and purpose in the fact that I am still here and able. . .to tell you what the Lord has done in my life. To be able to rejoice in what the Lord has done does not mean that all that has happened isn't painful, or that it no longer hurts. I still have nights where I cry myself to sleep. I still have panic attacks at pains that I get in my stomach, afraid that my cancer is back, or times where my sadness feels paralyzing. There are so many days that the most I'm going to get done is feed myself and exercise and play with my dog. And I've learned that that is okay, and that that is enough. I can still be thankful that I will get to live to see my friends get married, to become an aunt, and maybe eventually have a family, while simultaneously grieving the fact that I will never bear a child of my own. I can be both weak and strong at the same time.

My relationship with God has felt like a consistent push for Him to reach deeper inside me, to crack open rib by rib my pain, and fear, and sin. Each time I cry out in agony to Him, and each time His answer is simply "I know." And He really does know, because we have a God that walked among us and died for us so that we could be with Him. All He asks for in return is for us to love and trust Him. For me that looked like trusting Him with my life, for my family, that meant trusting Him with their daughter and sister. To be close to Jesus and to love is to understand suffering, because love on this earth is a suffering love.

I want to end with this last thought. In a show I recently watched, the main character is struggling with how to make sense of the pain and suffering that he and the people around him keep experiencing. As he talks to his friend about his confusions, she gives him this simple response. "I think that life is here to make us kinder. Because you have experienced pain, you can be kinder to people in ways that others cannot." She does not give him some long and philosophical explanation as to why his suffering is good— but rather, she shows him that despite what hurts him, despite what hurts all of us, we can choose to love one another because we know what it's like to feel alone. And honestly, I think sometimes life is as simple as that. If after all this, the result is I can pull back those bed sheets of shame for someone else and say, "Yes, this is really hard, but you're not alone," then I think I'm okay with just that.

Untitled

I am beginning to be convinced
To radically love
Despite how much it hurts
And it will hurt, expect it to
Just know
You will never read my poetry
I will never reach under the left side of my chest
And unhook what treasure lies beneath
You will never get the gift I was hoping to give
You could never hold a love as big as mine
You would hate me for it

Lover

I have sought arms like yours
since I was a child
Yes
I am still a child
still that child
that denied what was most desired
Lover
I saw you in a song
I waited for you by the water in white
white petals floating down around me
Sometimes it feels like you are worlds away
and I wonder if we'll ever meet
I want to stop grasping at what isn't there,
to stop hoping in what will not be given
but then again, maybe
it will one day appear before me
as if it had always been there
as if you had always been there
My love, my hope, my fear and resentment
does the way the song weaves such a nectar of sorrow and tenderness
strangle your heart, too
that it feels as though it will explode through your throat
Just so it can get the chance to say
"Yes I am here, I hear you"
My problem though
is that I'm afraid I will swallow back the swelling
in a facade of pride and protection
and miss my chance to be met
with what has been waiting for me all along

Untitled

You make me want to be honest
You make me wanna be good
Unearthed desires
I come up for air
but instead
Drown in tears
You taste like hope
Could someone like you
want to carry a grief such as mine?
I want to hope so
Cause I'm tired of killing inside
everything I want to feel
Show me the points of connection
I don't want to miss
what you've been trying to tell me
all along

Breadcrumbs

I keep finding pieces of you
that I don't remember inviting in
like the way a smile plays on my lips
at the thought of you saying
"I know your teeth"
as if it absurd that I would remind you
of the space that
reflects my mother's
or
how when I reached behind my bed
to a get a sock that had fallen
and out came your hat
with no trace of you left behind

how come love can leave such voids
so cavernous at times
I forget to come up for air
yet, in some contradicting way,
I seek its suffocation
almost daily
though, maybe,
what I'm searching for is
that same feeling of when I would drive home from work
knowing you were in bed waiting for me

what a beautiful thing to know that you consume someone's mind as
much as they have taken over yours

your name echoes

of a love lost to cowardice
and weak convictions
when I feel the curl of my lips once again at your memory
I remind myself
of the dead end your breadcrumbs led me to

I think I've finally stopped hoping that
you would once again
surprise me
with all that I've been waiting for

Untitled

Despite it all I will see the best parts of you and love them

Untitled

I will never be able to be with someone who views life as that simple,
because it's much bigger and sadder than just contentment.
Sometimes I think I made you out to be what I wanted for that time.
Then again, the way you put my socks on for me
could've made me cry.

Untitled

I will distance my heart
From what I can never have
so as to not cause my own aching
constantly
This kind of loss
is the kind you
can't just get over

Untitled

Life keeps breaking my heart
Again and again and again
So I cry
people tell me how strong I am
but let me tell you
I've never felt more vulnerable
then when I hold nothing back
Let me tell you
This body has known tragedy
so much so that, sometimes
I forget what it feels like to breathe new love in deeply
For I have not known a deeper heartache than what has been sowed
for a lifetime
Cherry blossoms with roots so deep,
though, I'm still waiting for the spring when they bloom
still asking when I can recklessly breathe deep again
without fear of what seeds will be scattered by such thoughtlessness
How can I?
when I'm still pruning my own branches,
In hopes of a respite
Sometimes
I think I don't know myself
beyond an existence of limbo
between what is here, and what has yet to be

Untitled

When there are things we have lost
To find is inevitable
Creation cannot begin without destruction
though what is being created may not be known to us
So go ahead
Grieve what has been taken
Mourn what you have lost
But take courage
and be comforted
for surely, something more beautiful has yet to be found

Untitled

You want me to feel empowered?
To feel strong as I stand before the world?
Then show me you love me
Never have I felt bolder
Than when you showed me
What those three words meant

Untitled

Sometimes I wanna scream to everyone
Look at what I carry
I'm alive
I'm alive
But, I've experienced such kindness that,
I tell you,
It could have softened the heart
of even my father
Could have told him
"It's okay, you're okay"
But that's something different entirely
Because he wasn't okay
and, sometimes,
I don't know if I will be
either
Except
"I'm alive
I'm alive"
I'm telling you
Kindness is born in the spaces
your pain has claimed
Suffering -
its womb

Untitled

Because of a denial of what I've wanted most, I blindly accepted cheap replacements without an emotional attachment. In denying my fear of desiring the genuine article, I subjected myself to sin and gross treatment as a means of a quick bandage—one that covered up a wound that still was festering, rather than cleaning it out first. By ignoring what was hurting, I only ended up creating more damage. Lord, please give me the grace and breath to receive your mercy and love, despite how repulsed by myself I feel. May your love cover it all.

Untitled

Embrace what is uncomfortable
I've been grasping at all the wrong things
When it turns out
I've been reaching for you all along

I Am Yours; Save Me

To live is to suffer (I am tired of suffering)
To love is to suffer (I grieve those I have yet to meet)

Their absence—the loss of them—
or, maybe,
"the possibility of not making it till they get here"
is the correct phrase.
Anyways,
I am grieving people
I have yet to know the names of;
some of whom, I will never know—
but that never knowing
is a thing of the past.

A thing of the past
that which now determines the future,
in which,
I am mourning
here in the present.

Which just goes to show you that
no matter how much you lie to yourself,
you will never escape life (suffering),
and the more you suffer (love),
doesn't always mean it'll be okay
in the end.

Which just goes to show you that
drinking coffee out of your favorite mug

every morning
is just as important
as working hard, or
holding the door for a stranger.

You deserve the common courtesy (love)
that the world so often
does not extend to you.

Untitled

I'm tired of my comfort being dependent on how much help I ask for

Untitled

What if, instead, strength made in our weakness is talking about how loved we are despite our weakest moments? That image of strength we create means nothing to God, nor does being loved in those "perfect" moments carry any weight. It's being loved even when we feel ashamed, broken, weak, and repulsed by our own selves. It's being seen by a God that wants to keep looking at us despite how badly we want everyone to get away from us.

Untitled

I'm holding out my bleeding heart in my hands
Begging someone to hear the way ribs crunch when they break open
But am met with silence
No one wants to meet me where I am and where this is hurting the most
No one is willing to take up my offering
As I bow my head and raise my hands
They drip from the freshness of my wounds
Cause, let's face it, this type of hurt is ongoing
And I'm not gonna pretend like I can do this on my own

Untitled

Do you know how many times I've fought this battle
Gone from skin and bones
To abundance?
It gets harder with each time

Untitled

It's nights like these
that I'm so scared of the monster that once was
that I'm (almost) unthankful to still be here
I want to hide under the covers
but instead
I'll call my mom—though
I'll still cover half of my face
with my t-shirt that says
"girls rock"

I'll be 24 in a week and a half
and I think, maybe, this is what it means to grow up—
realizing that those times you want to disappear
you should call your mom and cry, cry, cry
because, sometimes,
it feels like that monster is still here
waiting to catch you off guard
and only she knows how to say
"my honey, when you can't keep fighting, I will"

Untitled

Don't be afraid to ask to be picked up every now and again.

Untitled

Sometimes
I'll soap up a rag
and start cleaning—shoulder to palm—
instead of showering
and suddenly
I'm back at the hospital
as my mom takes the cloth under my chin
to my ear
the way
only a mom can do.
And just like that, I'm new again, even if it's
just for that moment.
What I'm trying to say is,
how do we ever move on
from the moments that defined us—
that made the parts of me
that exist in front of you now?

What It Means to Feel Empty

There is nothing poetic about life—
Except, maybe, that it continually ruins me
and I keep asking for more;
Or how things keep being ripped from within me,
so that I keep being emptied.
Yet, I still look for how to be filled.

I keep stitching up a festering wound and wonder why it won't quite
heal right.

If emptiness is a feeling
simply because I keep feeling it,
Then I guess it must be confronted
before I can fill it with what exactly it needs.
Or, maybe, it doesn't need to be filled at all.
Anyway, I'm beginning to think
I need to enter into
what no longer exists
before I can become.
Let me mourn what was taken
in order to finally let it go.

Though, sometimes, I don't think I really care
all that much.
But then I cry over trivial things like:
falling down the steps,
or a goat giving birth,
or my favorite manga character crying about
how empty he is.

I guess you don't know how strong you are
until you have no other choice,
but I disagree with that being strength.

What way of confronting (or avoiding) life would you consider to be weak,
and do you even have the privilege to make that judgment?

Honestly, I don't know what strength is anymore.
Because I keep crying about stupid goats,
and not being able to run fast enough,
and Erik Satie's Gymnopedie No. 1—
I don't know, just don't tell me I'm strong
when my only option was to endure.

Is it fair for me to not want to exist sometimes;
to want that hollowed-out heart feeling
to die alongside this strife?

Though, I think, what I really want
is for someone to notice
without me asking;
to say, "I feel empty too,
and I want you to know that doesn't mean
you're unable to fill anyone up."
I want someone to see my scar and start crying—
to trace from my heart,
to its half-moon around my mother's love,
to where it points to a silenced womb.

To not tell me how strong I am for enduring,
but that they're sorry I had to endure in the first place.

The Revolution I Never Wanted to Come

I'm scrambling to find meaning in everything.
The blinking light
far out in the distant ocean,
or
the plants that grow out of the concrete.
Maybe even
the wind that shakes my car as I sit here,
writing this,
and noticing all three of the above.

God tell me something, anything,
because I'm scared of this fight.
I never wanted to lead a revolution that I got thrown into—
never mind one I don't even know the purpose of.

How did I go from what I once was,
to whatever this is now?
How could you have let this happen to me?
How long am I going to feel like this?
I cried every night this week,
yet I find no relief—
no comfort in what it feels like to still live—
but can you even call this living?

Why do I have to do this?
Please don't make me do this.
I know I have to do this.

I'm still at the point where everything is a metaphor.

Open the window to get fresh air,
only to struggle to take in a breath—
I never seem to be able to keep up.

I'm at the point where breathing is an act of defiance,
eating is a taking up of arms,
and saying "I want to live"
is a war cry.
Come and listen to what has been declared over me by my God,
"We go until we can go no more."

Part Four

What's Inside Me Never Dies

The following was written by Kate.

Hanna wasn't here to write this last introduction, and so I am writing it for her. The previous introductions for Parts One, Two, and Three were taken from her senior testimony at Covenant College. After giving her testimony, Hanna lived a few more years before she died. In those years, she made every effort possible to re-enter life as a 20-something woman— and for a while, even if in the spirit of knowing deep down it was all on loan, she enjoyed the parts of herself that were seemingly returned to her. She moved back down to Tennessee and finished getting her college degree. She built her physical body back up to a strength that allowed her to return to the high-intensity training she loved so much and work as a training coach. She fell deeper in love with pottery and worked as a studio assistant for a ceramic artist she loved dearly. She continued to invest in friendships, dated a bit, visited friends that lived in other cities, and started dreaming again.

Looking back, we think she knew her time would be short after witnessing the sudden end of our father's walk with cancer, and that she was trying to fit in as much life as possible. After a little more than a year of being "cancer free," she went in for a routine scan and the doctors saw something. Even though they told us this type of cancer would eventually return, we didn't expect it to so quickly. The next step was to repeat her initial surgery, as the doctor was confident he would be able to remove any cancer the scan had shown.

Hanna then underwent the same surgery she described to you earlier in Part Two, only this time after cutting her so invasively open, the surgeon found her body to be riddled with tumors. The nature of this evil is that it had embedded itself in her tissue, making it impossible to remove. The only thing he could do was close her back up.

After she woke up from surgery, our mom walked into Hanna's recovery room prepared to once again give her daughter the worst news possible, only to be met by Hanna's words of comfort: "It's okay, I know. God told me He is going to take care of me." Hanna later had no recollection of saying this, and so we held on to it as a message of hope, wondering if it meant He was going to finally heal her. It turned out He would bring her healing, but not in the physical way we'd hoped for.

Hanna walked through her intense recovery for the second time, only this time there was no medical hope. In a last attempt to survive, she decided to try chemotherapy again, knowing that the chances it would help were slim to none. After a few rounds she decided to stop treatment, as the chemo made her so sick and left her with no quality of life for the short time she had left. For the remaining months of her life, Hanna managed her pain as best she could, and as the frailty of her body became more and more obvious, we watched a healing unfolding in her spirit—which is revealed in the following pages, her last writings.

Untitled

I wanna make sure I say the words
before I no longer can

Untitled

Elbows and knees bruised from begging
For one more minute, hour, day
I tell you
Mercy is a second breath

Untitled

Here's what I've learned of life:
That life keeps going
is the most painful
and beautiful part of it

Untitled

Disconnected
I reach and flail in every direction
But not really
And that's exactly the point

Untitled

Take me back to the time
Where I was ravenous for life
For beauty is still beauty
even if I can't have it

Untitled

I woke up and saw the sunrise
and thought
how beautiful it would be
to see it again and again.

Untitled

Summer
and its hot passions
have exhausted me
I am ready for the cool retreat
of fall
and winter's icy gnashes
hurrying you home
to the warmth of a found self
This winter I will once again
fall in love with myself

Untitled

There is a space
in which I
oscillate somewhere between
utter joy
and undeniable grief
It is a limbo,
a dance
of laughter amidst
welled eyes
where, somewhere,
I'm met by everyone
I have ever loved
or will ever love, where
the pitter patter of
a heart untethered
finds its breath

An Ode to Friendship

Everyone I have ever loved
Has kept one foot out
Everyone I have ever loved
Has held a silk thread attached to my tapestry with two fingers
But not you
No
You helped to weave it
See this part over here?
You started it
And this one here?
We made that together
And then there's this part that got a little messed up
Yet your thread never broke
I'm starting to think that this is what it means to love
To stay (when everyone else has gone)
To build (when everyone else keeps taking apart my foundation)
To pursue (when I am consumed by my own darkness)
Cause my tapestry has more than one mangled section
And it is sure to have many more
But because of you, I am not afraid to keep trying

Untitled

I liked when you called me your sister
Yes, it made me feel worthy of something more than casual shared
experiences of these passing days
That you saw me as more
That you not only allowed for me within the clouds
But welcomed it, desired it
Asking me to see the intricacies and shadows that were cast
While everyone was busy looking at the sun

Untitled

All is sweet and gentle
No, but all can be sweeter, gentler
Slower, softer

Untitled

Believe me when I tell you
that my heart breaks
daily
over the small caretaking
that happens
daily, like
a walk
a friend bringing food
rubbing your ma's swollen knee
There is more love
in the small, everyday trivialities
then any romance book
I've held

Untitled

Where the boy
with the hair like a crow
will meet me and,
at last,
I'll understand why
none before ever
seemed to fit quite right
How each one
was just a step closer to you
my bird, my heart

Untitled

As I find my body wasting away, the things I long for again surprise me. Things of my childhood: a walk in the woods in Maine as we walk to breakfast at Migis Lodge, the taste of their hot chocolate, the Friday night buffets where we all got dressed up and I'd order a virgin madras. I can clearly picture my father in one of his suits sitting on the back porch of the lodge while we waited to be seated and he drank a Stoli with club and lemon. The smell of the crisp, almost sweet, air of lake and pine trees still lingers in the back of my nose. These images and smells feel so enmeshed within my body lately that at times, it feels painful. I long for those days of mindless youth where the only thing that mattered was taking the next step forward to the next moment of life. A vacation that I can remember feeling (naively) inconvenienced by now displays itself to me in potent glimpses of shrub deserts and popover nights—fireplaces where we roasted marshmallows and the chess board where my father taught me to play. What I'm trying to say is that these small details of life—the commonplace, everyday lifting of hands and picking up feet—the tastes you adore but never bother to think twice about because you don't need to—these are the things I want back. These are the things my body craves. These are the things that feel agonizingly unattainable, yet beautiful and perfect. They fill me with immense gratitude and longing, so much so that at times I think my heart is going to inflate straight out of my chest and lift me away to take me back.

What I Mean When I Say That I'm Happy

What I mean when I say that I'm happy
is that
making my sister laugh
still feels like I'm the funniest person ever
and that my dog
is still one of my favorite smells
and that I'll never get sick of swimming in the ocean.

See, I'm trying to explain
that feeling of a sunny day
with friends that somehow make time go
both faster and in reverse
but in a way that makes you say
"this is home."

I'm trying to explain
that I will never get sick of
those days with the ones you love
when I can be most myself
that is when I am most alive.

What I'm trying to say is
how can I feel so alive
when everything is telling me
I shouldn't be?

I mean,
Life is beautiful
and I have more time

I have to have more time
I want more time
I am ready for more.

I think God has been talking to me all along.

Conversation with the Crows

I watched the child,
hair like crow's feathers,
chase his little brother across the grass
—the light was cloaked in a hazy grey blanket that day—
and I thought,
this is what beauty is,
this is what it means to be alive.
You saw it too
and though, so simple,
I felt I finally understood
what a helpless feeling awe is.
And as the music welled up within my head,
so did my chest.
Who was I to have just experienced such truth?
to have breathed that same, grey air
as a child that once belonged to a crow
that once belonged (still belongs) to a God
who saw it all
I tell you,
you don't know what it means to be alive
until you might have to give it up—
When, some months later,
you are reminded
of freedom, and wet air, and feathers
and you are thankful just to have
seen,
heard,
felt, such commonplace things,
though,
they are but what makes up the whole

Untitled

I miss when I could pull the towel over my shoulders
after a shower.
Now, I wrap it across my breasts
hiding everything that's beneath
afraid of what can be seen.
I miss when such shame didn't exist.

Lemon Italian Ice

Body,
Vessel of my being
Container of my sorrow and gratitude—
with hair that keeps growing
and hands that keep reaching,
does it hurt to know you'll never stop trying to live?

Body,
Let me give you what you love
like
the smell of your dog,
or
ocean water on your lips
and skin on a hot day,
or
your favorite Italian ice
on a day you cried too much.
Lemon tastes like being little.

Body,
I promise I love you
even on days when I don't.
I'll say it again,
I love you
even when tenderness
is the last thing on our mind.

Body,
I promise I'm trying

(I'm trying I'm trying)
trying to get it right,
trying to hold you
when no one else can,
because, let's face it,
how can anyone understand
like we can?

Body,
How I wish I could grow old with you,
nourish you
to our one heart's content
instead of taking
hit
after hit
after hit.
How many more times will I apologize?
(I'm sorry I'm sorry);
Just know I'll keep going
for us.

Body,
Is it okay to dream again?
Is it okay
to hold each other in grace
and adoration,
and see what we have hoped for
all along?

Body,
In all your complexities,

help me to see the parts
that have flourished.
Let me speak peace over you,
comfort for your hunger,
and satisfaction for your thirst
as we no longer rage within
what is left
of our existence.

How Do We Comfort the Ones We Will One Day Leave Behind?

I tell my mom lies a lot
like
I already walked the dog
and
I'll clean my room in 10 minutes
and
I'm gonna be here for a while.

How do I comfort my mother
when only my presence
fixes my coming absence?
How do I hold her
when I'm gone?
How do I tell her
"It'll all be okay"
when, in fact,
this is getting worse
and I am getting tired.

How do I tell her
to keep my dog
to have my best friend
over for dinner still;
to keep watching
our favorite shows
even if I can't be there.

What I am asking is
how do I tell my mom
to keep living,
and hold these parts of me
when the whole can no longer, hold her
How do I tell my mother
to live
when I am dying?

Untitled

To return to the earth
from which you came,
how beautiful to think
that my last gift to the world
will be
myself.

Therapeutic Writing Exercise

An Encouragement to Create from Kate

Dear Friend,

I HOPE AND PRAY MY SISTER'S WRITINGS MEET YOU where you most need to be met—in your highest highs and lowest lows, and most especially in the places you may not want to even go. May her honesty and vulnerability give you permission to let out what is in your heart. At this point I would like to invite you into the healing process of writing your own poetry. I believe this exercise will bring you emotional and physical relief, a sense of connection to your Creator, and allow you to feel more at home in your body. You do not need to be creative or skilled with words to partake in this process. All you need to be able to do is write. If you cannot physically write, ask someone to write down what you speak out to them. Hello, spoken word poetry!

Where I'm Coming From

I believe strongly in the healing benefits of making art, especially when it's done in a life-giving community. Walls come down, truth is told and a well of creativity is tapped into when we create from a place of genuine curiosity and diversity. My main art practices are weaving and natural dyeing. I love both because they force me to slow down, settle into my body and allow me to process emotions in a safe environment. I am the one setting the speed, taking breaks when I need to, pushing myself to sit a bit longer, and do the work when I feel I can. I've learned to trust myself and the process; that working with my hands and allowing myself to get what's on the inside out is important and meaningful work.

Aside from my own ongoing healing journey, I am most passionate about creating safe spaces for others to experience the healing benefits of making art. I love when God calls my attention to someone's gifting and gives me the opportunity to call it out in them; to encourage and empower them to chase after what's on their heart. I believe we have a responsibility to develop the person we were created to be and to have respect for the way we were made. There will always be outside forces speaking lies to you— "it's too late to start now," "you're not capable," "you have nothing of value to say." Those lies can be paralyzing, and until you realize that they have no actual authority over you— they will try to keep you from sharing the message you carry, your glorious treasure within (2 Corinthians 4:7 TPT). I truly believe that where we feel the most opposition, we find the calling on our lives.

When I teach weaving workshops, I like to keep the call to create very open to whatever each person is carrying and needs to get out. I'm not an art therapist, but I have been trained in studio art therapy—the difference being that there are no medical or diagnostic aspects to my leadership role. I am there to create a safe space for people to come and use provided materials to make art. I don't give clinical feedback; I hold space, answer technical questions and encourage the artist to go after whatever it is they have in their heart to create.

I start each series by sharing a bit about myself, my introduction to the craft at hand, and how it's impacted my life. Then I show some weaving samples, enough to show technique and possibility, but few enough to not impose my personal aesthetic and interpretation onto anyone. Next, I teach the foundational weaving skills so each person's piece will be structurally sound once it's finished. After that, I try to get out of the way as much as possible.

When I first started, I was perfectionistic and controlling about it all, but I quickly realized that it was unnecessary, hindering the process actually. It was effective and my presentation was beautiful, but I felt like the spirit of perfectionism and control would flow out of me and affect the art-making of the students, and so I let it all go. Once I did, it was incredible how much more life-giving our time was together. I honestly think that no one else noticed the difference, however, I knew it was a necessary shift I needed to make for all of us.

In sharing this, I ask you to let go of trying to do this exercise "the right way." You will probably start out in a perfectionistic and controlling way, and I want to give you permission to move through that and let go and just see what comes out of you. I'm going to ask you a few questions to help settle you in. Then I'll go first and share a poem I wrote for Hanna, inspired by how openly she shared her own poetry. I was surprised by how therapeutic it was for me; bringing emotional and physical relief, and giving me the opportunity to share a message that was difficult to express in conversational language. I believe you will have the same experience in writing your own poetry.

Settling In

Before we start, I invite you to do whatever helps you feel more grounded. Maybe you sit in silence for a few minutes. Maybe you light a candle to acknowledge and honor the time you're taking for yourself. Maybe you are like me and you just want to jump right in. One thing I like to do is say a prayer, something short and sweet because I am usually impatient and come to the exercise pretty desperate to make sense of and get out all that is going on inside of me. My prayer is usually along the lines of, "God please help me, be with me, speak to me, I need you." And then I start to write.

Sometimes it's a pouring out of the chaos inside my head; the kind of stuff you never want to read after writing it. (The good news is, you don't have to.) Other times, when I am feeling so vulnerable and sensitive and completely undone, my writing reflects the structure of an even simpler prayer, when I have no words to pray beyond "Jesus." That's the place I'm talking about. It's in this place that I write what I'll call poetry. Don't worry about your spelling, grammar, the structure, or continuity of the thoughts you're putting down. Just let it flow out of you and see how you feel.

Some Questions to Help You Get Started

As Hanna's physical body got weaker, her senses heightened and the world around her came alive in the way it only does for those nearing Heaven. I've heard it explained that as we near death, the veil between Heaven and Earth thins out, and our ability to taste, hear, see, smell, and feel moves towards restoration of their original design upon our creation before sin entered in.

Hanna often talked and wrote about specific sensory memories, many of which were from her childhood. When she could no longer leave my mom's house, you could find her on the back porch sitting cozily on a sheep skin donned wicker chair by the fire pit in silence, peacefully listening to the wind blow through the trees. I'd sit down beside her and she'd call my attention to the sound and tell me how it is one of her most favorite sounds in the world, especially when it's accompanied by the smell of a wood-burning fire. There was the fact that her world was getting smaller the sicker she got, but I also saw how much more expansive and beautiful and true her world got as the veil thinned.

Now it's time I give you some writing prompts—inspired by my conversations with Hanna around the fire pit, while the trees blew softly in the wind. My hope is that they get you started and the writing flows more effortlessly after going through them.

Write down some words that describe how you are feeling right now.

What do you smell in this moment? Does it bring any memories to mind?

What is the temperature like where you are? Do you feel hot, warm, or cold?

Does your body feel tense or relaxed? Where do you feel the tension?

What are some of your favorite sounds? Why?

What colors do you see? Can you feel them in any specific parts of your body?

What colors would you use to describe how you feel right now? Why?

What meal most makes you feel like you are home? Who cooks/cooked it for you?

What season would you use to describe how you feel right now (summer, fall, winter, spring)? Why?

What flower would you use to describe how you feel right now? Why?

Who, in the course of your life, has made you feel loved?

I'LL GO FIRST

For anyone who feels uneasy about writing poetry, I thought that I would go first and share with you a poem that I wrote based on these prompts. I wrote it on a last-minute-decision plane ride back to New Jersey to surprise Hanna for her last birthday, while my baby slept in the cot at my feet. My body and mind were flooded with emotion, and I didn't know what else to do. So, I took note from my sister and started to write. I cried while writing it, and I felt some relief after finishing it. I hope it encourages you to get started on your own writing and that you find some relief in your process.

A Dove Named Blossom

You are like the dove
who brought back the olive branch;
a carrier of Hope, of Love, eternal.

You are like the dove
who brought back the olive branch,
except you carry something much more fitting to you.
You, you carry a cherry blossom branch
and with it, you've brought heaven
to earth.

The Grace in your suffering.
The Humility in your posture.
The Life in your lack.
The Savior in your savor.

Sick in front of us,
your body broken open—
we watch as His love pours out
onto all of us.
It makes no sense on earth but
the sicker you get—
your spirit, it blossoms.
Less of you, more of Him, blossoms.

And you,
you are beautiful,
Blossom.

YOUR TURN

I hope you enter into this part of the writing exercise knowing that writing is a beautiful and brave thing to do. I hope you are proud of yourself for stepping outside of your comfort zone—for putting down on paper all that you've been carrying. I am very proud of you, and I have one ask: Would you share one thing you write with someone else? If you're not ready to share with another person, would you read it to a pet? If you don't have a pet, would you read it out loud to yourself? Sometimes, I'll read out loud what I've written and it affects me in a totally different way than it did while writing it. I also find it helps me to have compassion for myself, as if I'm hearing someone else's story. As you continue in your writing journey, I hope you invite others into it—to hear your words, your story, your thoughts. As I said to Hanna, you never know who needs to hear what you have to say.

Kate & Hanna

ABOUT THE AUTHORS

HANNA WILT IS THE AUTHOR AND POET OF *I Would Live For You*. Hanna was a fiercely loyal friend, a truth-teller, and a warrior of light with the heart of an artist. She graduated from Covenant College with a degree in Interdisciplinary Studies—focusing on Art, Psychology and Biology. Hanna lived and worked in Tennessee as a Studio Assistant for a Ceramic Artist and as a Crossfit Coach. She moved home to New Jersey as her health declined to be close to family and receive proper care. Hanna died on Valentine's Day—February 14, 2022, at the age of 27 after battling Mesothelioma for years.

Hanna dreamt of publishing her poetry in hopes of leaving behind a tangible legacy— one that would help others going through similar suffering to know that they are not alone; that a friend has gone before them and that she wants to help carry their sorrow.

KATE KIESEL IS AN ARTIST AND HANNA'S SISTER. Her practice includes handweaving and natural dyeing. With a background in fashion, Kate left the industry to pursue a more sustainable and holistic approach to the arts. That brought her to the Textile Arts Center in Brooklyn, NY, where she worked as an apprentice to the head weaver and designer.

Kate is trained in studio art therapy and strongly believes in the power of creating safe spaces for others to experience the healing benefits of making art in community. She taught weaving workshops to her local community and worked as a weaving instructor and animal caretaker at OASIS, tlc, a therapeutic farm for young adults with Autism before moving to Germany. She currently lives and works out of her home studio in Germany with her husband Tobias, and their two children, Leopold and Junia.

WE WOULD LOVE TO CONNECT WITH YOU

Hanna wrote these poems for herself first and foremost, but she chose to share them publicly in hopes that someone would connect with her writing and feel they had a friend alongside them in their walk through grief and acceptance. We, her family, would love to hear if this book has impacted you. Please visit us at **hannawilt.com** and leave a note of your experience if you feel led.

We believe that God brings comfort and healing through testimony and also through art. In Hanna's life, He brought both through poetry. We see this book as a carrier of comfort and healing; and dream of it helping others in similar seasons of life. If you work in hospice, as a death doula, as a grief counselor, or in a similar caretaking role and would like to order copies of this book in bulk, we would like to make it possible for you to get what you need. Please reach out via **hannawilt.com**.

My family and I have needed people to come alongside us and help walk us through the grief and acceptance of losing our loved ones. Sometimes those people are our real-life friends and sometimes they are those who feel like friends when we read their books or listen to their podcasts. Here are some books my family and I find helpful in our own walks through grief and acceptance.

A Grace Disguised by Jerry Sitter

The Loveliness of Christ by Samuel Rutherford

Out of the Depths by Oscar Wilde

Surviving the Tsunami of Grief by Katrina Taee and Wendelien McNicoll

God's Grace in your Suffering by David Powlison

Embodied Hope by Kelly M. Kapic

Everything You Have Ever Wanted to Know about Heaven— But Never Dreamed of Asking by Peter Kreeft

This Too Shall Last: Finding Grace When Suffering Lingers by K.J. Ramsey

Everything Happens Podcast with Kate Bowler

KATE'S GRATITUDES

This book was alive well before I pieced it together—poems lighting up and asking to be seated next to each other as I sat with piles of them around me. I could not have done the work had it not been for the Holy Spirit working through me and the wonderful people who entered into my sister's story and this project of ours. I'm so grateful for the following people and their help along the way. Without them this book would not exist.

Hanna Wilt- Thank you for sharing your heart and your story so vulnerably. Your words carry the oil produced in your suffering. What a costly gift you've given us. I am forever marked by your trust in me to bring this book to life. I can't wait to see you again and hear what you think about it.

Hope Wilt- Mama, thank you for always laying down your life for your children. I'm learning the dance that the tension between joy and grief requires with my own kids— and you did it for six of us. Thank you for taking such beautiful care of Hanna. She was never in it alone with you, her best friend, by her side. You stopped your world to enter fully into hers and I'll always admire how fiercely you protected, cared for and carried her when she needed it the most. You walked our Hanna home better than anyone else could—all while cooking and baking everything her heart desired no matter the time of day or night.

Tobias Kiesel- My love, thank you for walking out these past few years of grief alongside me. You came back into my life as everything started to fall apart and I'm so grateful for your steady presence through it all. Thank you for initiating all of the many trips back to the States, and for insisting we go when I said I couldn't do it again. Each time it was your idea that we go and be with my sister and my family—dafür ich liebe dich so sehr.

Joanna Jelley- Jojo, from school papers to interviews to crowdfunding miracles to this beautiful book—look how far we've come.

Thank you for always being my personal editor and for answering my phone calls even when you're at Costco. I'm sorry Natalie and I tried to get you fired so many times back in the day.

Megan Faulkner- What a dreamgirl sister friend you are. Thank you for always checking in, encouraging me along the way and sharing with me your own book-writing journey. Of course God would give us the gift of sharing in this journey together. He must love us a lot.

Michael Johnson- What a sacred gift you gave our family in painting the cherry blossoms that cover this book and hang in Hanna's bedroom. Your and Cheyenne's willingness to enter into our tragedy and hold Hanna's story with such sensitivity is an act of love we will never forget. Thank you for honoring Hanna with your artist's heart and for stewarding the gifts our God has given you so well. I know He is so proud of you.

Joy and Amelia at Punchline Agency- I don't believe I could have brought this book to life without you two. I know I could not have done it in such a short amount of time. I had no idea what I was doing and you really did make it fun! Thank you for investing your wealth of knowledge, your time and your generosity into this project. Thank you for believing it is special and worthy to be shared with the world.

Kristin McNess Moran- Thank you for treating this project so tenderly, for designing it with such care and talent. Thank you for sharing with me about your own loss. I'm so grateful you're the one I got to design this book with.

A NOTE FROM THE COVER ARTIST

In the month of January 2022, several weeks before Hanna passed, I made a painting called Agony. The painting is of a thin stalk of a sunflower, scorched by winter, suspended in the posture of a crucifixion. I posted images of the painting on social media and addressed the painting to those experiencing grief of any kind. Hanna had followed my account a few weeks prior. A few days after I posted Agony, Hanna posted an image of a painting of a different kind—it was of pink clouds and a distant figure on a green hill with a little house. It was serene and comforting and calm. When I saw this, I had a revelation and felt humbled, almost ashamed. There I was, in a state of relative physical health, making a painting called Agony, while Hanna who was in true physical anguish was sharing comforting images of pink clouds. I reflected on this for a few days. And then, out of the blue, Hanna reached out to me with her sister Kate, and asked if I would paint cherry blossoms. The painting would be a gift for her mom, Hope, and the image of the painting would be the cover of her book, to be published posthumously. At this request I experienced a second revelation: Hanna wanted the painter who painted Agony to paint the pink clouds, so to speak. I accepted the task with humility.

The supplies for the painting arrived at my door the night before Hanna passed away. I made the frame and stretched the canvas before going to bed that night. I think I was hoping that if I worked quickly enough Hanna would be able to see the painting. But in truth, Hanna was to be my guide presiding over the work from the realm of spirit. During the first days of the work, I was walking down a sidewalk and suddenly at my feet were a tuft of faux pink cherry blossoms. I picked them up and put them in my pocket, carried them home and kept them on my palette for the duration of the painting.

I remember a few weeks into the work I was encountering some technical difficulty and experiencing doubt about the direction of the painting. I went for a walk with my fiancée, Cheyenne, and in response to my doubts, Cheyenne said, "well, why don't you talk to Hanna about it?" When we got back home, I typed Hanna's name into the search bar and found her speech from Covenant College. I was deeply moved. Her strength and wisdom and the way her voice nearly trembled as she spoke her truth had the effect on me of banishing all doubt and confusion—the work unfolded from that point on with renewed clarity and intent.

What I learned is that the work of art can honor human suffering and register as simple beauty. The work doesn't have to be "about" suffering in order to reach the sufferer. The same way van Gogh's sunflowers can speak of loneliness, one can honor human suffering with the brush stoke of a cherry blossom. "Suffering & joy are not opposites but can both exist in the same moment in a way that only grace allows," as Hanna puts it. The title for the painting arrived near the end of the process, while I was reading *He Held Radical Light: The Art of Faith, the Faith of Art* by Christian Wiman—a poet who went through his own battle with cancer. He tells a story of the poet Seamus Heaney who's last words before he died were a text sent to his wife that said, "Noli Timere," or, "Be Not Afraid."

I pray that Hanna likes the painting and that my work has been faithful. I thank her and believe her request has been a true blessing. I thank her sister Kate for being the connective weaver that brought us all together to work on this project. I thank her brother, Sam, for the conversations we had while I painted. I don't see cherry blossoms the same anymore, and I'm very grateful for that.

- Michael J. Johnson

ABOUT THE WOMEN WHO HELPED BRING THIS BOOK TO LIFE

Joy Eggerichs Reed resides as an expat in Paris, France with her husband Matt and two petite bébés, Millie and Emerson. She is the founder of Punchline Agency: A literary and speaking agency for people good on the page and stage. She loves working with communicators and people who want to get their words into the world — in whatever form. She also has found her own voice and authored two books on writing. One for adults and one for children. One of her greatest honors in doing this work has been to help Kate get Hanna's poetry out into the world and to witness the undying love and loyalty of one sister to another.

Amelia Graves is the Literary Assistant and Editor at Punchline Agency. Though her days are spent working with words and powerful writers, she also loves to be outside and explore her beautiful home state of Colorado with her dog, Pepper. Amelia's work is driven by a quote from Patti Digh: "The shortest distance between two people is a story." Her goal as an editor is to help authors communicate their stories to audiences in a way that is true, connecting, and unique. Amelia was particularly moved by Hanna's writing and ability to so beautifully share her changing understanding of life, loss, love, family, and faith, and is honored to be a part of this project.

Kristin McNess Moran is an illustrator, designer, and maker living in Portland, Oregon. After 10 years working as an apparel designer at Adidas, she now thrives in making a variety of creative endeavors come to life such as illustrating picture books like *Buzz the Not-So-Brave*, designing covers and book interiors for independent authors, and crafting costumes for her two daughters and good-sport of a husband at Halloween. She credits much of her artistic talent to her father, an accomplished architect and designer, whose recent passing made this project with Kate extra special. It is truly an honor to work on the book.

BIBLIOGRAPHY

Kreeft, Peter. *Everything You Ever Wanted to Know About Heaven: But Never Dreamed of Asking.* San Francisco: Ignatius Press, 1990.

"We are like common clay jars that carry this glorious treasure within, so that this immeasurable power will be seen as God's, not ours. Though we experience every kind of pressure, we're not crushed. At times we don't know what to do, but quitting is not an option. We are persecuted by others, but God has not forsaken us. We may be knocked down, but not out. We continually share in the death of Jesus in our own bodies so that the resurrection life of Jesus will be revealed through our humanity. We consider living to mean that we are constantly being handed over to death for Jesus' sake so that the life of Jesus will be revealed through our humanity. So, then, death is at work in us but it releases life in you.

We have the same Spirit of faith that is described in the Scriptures when it says,

'First I believed, then I spoke in faith.'

So we also first believe then speak in faith. We do this because we are convinced that he who raised Jesus will raise us up with him, and together we will all be brought into his presence. Yes, all things work for your enrichment so that more of God's marvelous grace will spread to more and more people, resulting in an even greater increase of praise to God, bringing him even more glory!

So no wonder we don't give up. For even though our outer person gradually wears out, our inner being is renewed every single day. We view our slight, short-lived troubles in the light of eternity. We see our difficulties as the substance that produces for us an eternal, weighty glory far beyond all comparison, because we don't focus our attention on what is seen but on what is unseen. For what is seen is temporary, but the unseen realm is eternal."

2 Corinthians 4:7-18 TPT

Made in United States
North Haven, CT
17 July 2023